50 Grain-Free Baking with Nut Recipes for Home

By: Kelly Johnson

Table of Contents

- Almond Flour Banana Bread
- Paleo Chocolate Chip Cookies
- Walnut Zucchini Bread
- Cashew Butter Brownies
- Coconut Flour Pancakes
- Hazelnut Muffins
- Pecan Pie Bars
- Macadamia Nut Biscotti
- Sunflower Seed Crackers
- Pistachio Lemon Bars
- Sesame Seed Breadsticks
- Pine Nut Energy Balls
- Brazil Nut Fudge
- Pumpkin Seed Bread
- Almond Joy Bites
- Walnut Flour Waffles
- Cashew Cream Frosting
- Coconut Macaroons
- Hazelnut Chocolate Spread
- Pecan Butter Cookies
- Macadamia Nut Granola
- Sunflower Seed Bread
- Pistachio Rosewater Cake
- Sesame Seed Cookies
- Pine Nut Pesto Pizza Crust
- Brazil Nut Truffles
- Pumpkin Seed Crackers
- Almond Flour Biscuits
- Walnut Date Bars
- Cashew Cheesecake
- Coconut Flour Tortillas
- Hazelnut Crusted Chicken Tenders
- Pecan Crumble Apple Pie
- Macadamia Nut-Crusted Fish
- Sunflower Seed Salad Dressing

- Pistachio Crusted Salmon
- Sesame Seed Chicken Tenders
- Pine Nut Hummus
- Brazil Nut Crusted Pork Chops
- Pumpkin Seed Pesto Pasta
- Almond Flour Pizza Crust
- Walnut Encrusted Goat Cheese Balls
- Cashew Alfredo Sauce
- Coconut Flour Fried Chicken
- Hazelnut-Crusted Tofu
- Pecan-Crusted Eggplant
- Macadamia Nut Salad Toppings
- Sunflower Seed Encrusted Pork Tenderloin
- Pistachio Crusted Goat Cheese
- Sesame Seed Coated Shrimp

Almond Flour Banana Bread

Ingredients:

- 3 ripe bananas
- 3 eggs
- 1/4 cup melted coconut oil or butter
- 1/4 cup honey or maple syrup (adjust to taste)
- 1 teaspoon vanilla extract
- 2 cups almond flour
- 1 teaspoon baking powder
- 1/2 teaspoon baking soda
- 1/2 teaspoon salt
- Optional: 1/2 cup chopped nuts or chocolate chips

Instructions:

Preheat your oven to 350°F (175°C). Grease a loaf pan or line it with parchment paper.
In a mixing bowl, mash the ripe bananas with a fork until smooth.
Add the eggs, melted coconut oil or butter, honey or maple syrup, and vanilla extract to the mashed bananas. Mix until well combined.
In a separate bowl, whisk together the almond flour, baking powder, baking soda, and salt.
Gradually add the dry ingredients to the wet ingredients, stirring until just combined. Be careful not to overmix.
If desired, fold in chopped nuts or chocolate chips.
Pour the batter into the prepared loaf pan and spread it evenly.
Bake in the preheated oven for 50-60 minutes, or until a toothpick inserted into the center comes out clean.
Once baked, remove the banana bread from the oven and allow it to cool in the pan for 10-15 minutes.
Transfer the bread to a wire rack to cool completely before slicing and serving.

Enjoy your homemade almond flour banana bread! It's perfect for breakfast, snack time, or dessert.

Paleo Chocolate Chip Cookies

Ingredients:
- 2 cups almond flour
- 1/4 cup coconut flour
- 1/2 teaspoon baking soda
- 1/4 teaspoon salt
- 1/3 cup coconut oil, melted
- 1/3 cup honey or maple syrup
- 2 teaspoons vanilla extract
- 1/2 cup dairy-free chocolate chips

Instructions:

Preheat your oven to 350°F (175°C). Line a baking sheet with parchment paper.
In a large mixing bowl, combine the almond flour, coconut flour, baking soda, and salt.
In a separate bowl, whisk together the melted coconut oil, honey or maple syrup, and vanilla extract until well combined.
Gradually add the wet ingredients to the dry ingredients, stirring until a dough forms.
Fold in the chocolate chips until evenly distributed throughout the dough.
Use a cookie scoop or tablespoon to scoop out dough and roll it into balls. Place the dough balls onto the prepared baking sheet, leaving some space between each cookie.
Use a fork to gently flatten each cookie slightly.
Bake in the preheated oven for 10-12 minutes, or until the edges are golden brown.
Remove the cookies from the oven and let them cool on the baking sheet for a few minutes before transferring them to a wire rack to cool completely.
Once cooled, store the paleo chocolate chip cookies in an airtight container at room temperature for up to 5 days.

Enjoy your delicious paleo chocolate chip cookies guilt-free! They're perfect for satisfying your sweet tooth while sticking to your dietary preferences.

Walnut Zucchini Bread

Ingredients:

- 2 cups shredded zucchini (about 2 medium zucchinis)
- 2 cups all-purpose flour or whole wheat flour
- 1 teaspoon baking soda
- 1/2 teaspoon baking powder
- 1/2 teaspoon salt
- 1 teaspoon ground cinnamon
- 1/2 teaspoon ground nutmeg
- 1/2 cup granulated sugar
- 1/2 cup brown sugar, packed
- 1/2 cup unsweetened applesauce
- 1/3 cup vegetable oil or melted coconut oil
- 2 large eggs
- 1 teaspoon vanilla extract
- 1 cup chopped walnuts (optional)

Instructions:

Preheat your oven to 350°F (175°C). Grease a 9x5-inch loaf pan or line it with parchment paper.

Place the shredded zucchini in a clean kitchen towel and squeeze out excess moisture. Set aside.

In a large mixing bowl, whisk together the flour, baking soda, baking powder, salt, cinnamon, and nutmeg.

In another bowl, whisk together the granulated sugar, brown sugar, applesauce, oil, eggs, and vanilla extract until well combined.

Add the wet ingredients to the dry ingredients and stir until just combined. Avoid overmixing.

Fold in the shredded zucchini and chopped walnuts until evenly distributed throughout the batter.

Pour the batter into the prepared loaf pan and spread it evenly.

Bake in the preheated oven for 50-60 minutes, or until a toothpick inserted into the center comes out clean.

If the top of the bread starts to brown too quickly, you can cover it loosely with aluminum foil during the last 15-20 minutes of baking.

Once baked, remove the zucchini bread from the oven and allow it to cool in the pan for 10-15 minutes before transferring it to a wire rack to cool completely.

Slice and serve the walnut zucchini bread once it has cooled to your desired temperature.

Enjoy your homemade walnut zucchini bread as a tasty breakfast treat or snack!

Cashew Butter Brownies

Ingredients:

- 1 cup cashew butter
- 1/2 cup maple syrup or honey
- 2 large eggs
- 1 teaspoon vanilla extract
- 1/4 cup cocoa powder
- 1/2 teaspoon baking soda
- 1/4 teaspoon salt
- 1/2 cup chocolate chips (optional)

Instructions:

Preheat your oven to 350°F (175°C). Grease an 8x8 inch baking dish or line it with parchment paper.

In a mixing bowl, combine the cashew butter, maple syrup or honey, eggs, and vanilla extract. Stir until well combined and smooth.

Add the cocoa powder, baking soda, and salt to the cashew butter mixture. Stir until fully incorporated.

If desired, fold in the chocolate chips.

Pour the batter into the prepared baking dish and spread it out evenly.

Bake in the preheated oven for 20-25 minutes, or until the brownies are set and a toothpick inserted into the center comes out with a few moist crumbs.

Remove the brownies from the oven and let them cool in the pan for at least 15 minutes before slicing.

Once cooled, slice the brownies into squares and serve.

These cashew butter brownies are rich, fudgy, and utterly delicious. Enjoy them as a treat for yourself or share them with friends and family!

Coconut Flour Pancakes

Ingredients:

- 4 large eggs
- 1/2 cup coconut milk (or any milk of your choice)
- 2 tablespoons melted coconut oil (or butter), plus more for cooking
- 1 teaspoon vanilla extract
- 1/4 cup coconut flour
- 1 teaspoon baking powder
- Pinch of salt
- Optional: sweetener of your choice (such as honey, maple syrup, or stevia) to taste

Instructions:

In a mixing bowl, whisk together the eggs, coconut milk, melted coconut oil (or butter), and vanilla extract until well combined.

In a separate bowl, combine the coconut flour, baking powder, and salt.

Gradually add the dry ingredients to the wet ingredients, stirring until a smooth batter forms. If the batter is too thick, you can add a little more milk to reach your desired consistency. If you're using a sweetener, add it to the batter now and adjust to taste.

Heat a skillet or frying pan over medium heat and lightly grease it with coconut oil or butter.

Once the pan is hot, pour a small amount of batter onto the skillet to form pancakes of your desired size. Use the back of a spoon to spread the batter into a round shape.

Cook the pancakes for 2-3 minutes, or until bubbles form on the surface and the edges begin to look set.

Carefully flip the pancakes and cook for an additional 1-2 minutes on the other side, until golden brown and cooked through.

Transfer the cooked pancakes to a plate and repeat the process with the remaining batter, greasing the pan as needed between batches.

Serve the coconut flour pancakes warm, topped with your favorite toppings such as fresh fruit, maple syrup, nut butter, or coconut yogurt.

Enjoy your delicious and fluffy coconut flour pancakes for a wholesome breakfast or brunch!

Hazelnut Muffins

Ingredients:

- 1 3/4 cups all-purpose flour
- 1/2 cup granulated sugar
- 1/2 cup chopped hazelnuts
- 2 teaspoons baking powder
- 1/2 teaspoon salt
- 1/2 cup milk
- 1/2 cup unsalted butter, melted
- 2 large eggs
- 1 teaspoon vanilla extract

Instructions:

Preheat your oven to 375°F (190°C). Line a muffin tin with paper liners or grease the cups lightly with butter or cooking spray.
In a large mixing bowl, combine the flour, sugar, chopped hazelnuts, baking powder, and salt. Stir well to ensure even distribution of ingredients.
In another bowl, whisk together the milk, melted butter, eggs, and vanilla extract until smooth.
Pour the wet ingredients into the dry ingredients and stir gently until just combined. Be careful not to overmix; a few lumps are okay.
Spoon the batter into the prepared muffin cups, filling each about two-thirds full.
Optional: Sprinkle some additional chopped hazelnuts on top of each muffin for extra crunch and flavor.
Bake in the preheated oven for 18-20 minutes, or until the muffins are golden brown and a toothpick inserted into the center comes out clean.
Once baked, remove the muffins from the oven and let them cool in the pan for a few minutes before transferring them to a wire rack to cool completely.
Serve the hazelnut muffins warm or at room temperature. Enjoy with a cup of coffee or tea for a delightful treat!

Feel free to adjust the sweetness or add other ingredients like chocolate chips or dried fruit to customize the muffins to your liking. Enjoy your homemade hazelnut muffins!

Pecan Pie Bars

Ingredients:

For the Crust:

- 1 1/2 cups all-purpose flour
- 1/2 cup confectioners' sugar
- 3/4 cup unsalted butter, cold and cubed

For the Pecan Filling:

- 3/4 cup unsalted butter
- 1 cup packed light brown sugar
- 1/3 cup honey or maple syrup
- 2 tablespoons heavy cream
- 4 cups pecan halves

Instructions:

1. Preheat the Oven:

Preheat your oven to 350°F (175°C). Grease a 9x13-inch baking dish or line it with parchment paper, leaving an overhang on the sides for easy removal.

2. Make the Crust:
   - In a mixing bowl, combine the flour and confectioners' sugar.
   - Cut in the cold butter using a pastry cutter or two knives until the mixture resembles coarse crumbs.
   - Press the mixture evenly into the bottom of the prepared baking dish.
   - Bake the crust in the preheated oven for 18-20 minutes, or until lightly golden.

3. Prepare the Pecan Filling:
   - In a saucepan over medium heat, melt the butter.
   - Stir in the brown sugar, honey or maple syrup, and heavy cream. Cook, stirring constantly, until the mixture comes to a boil.
   - Remove the saucepan from the heat and stir in the pecan halves until evenly coated.

4. Assemble and Bake:

    - Pour the pecan filling evenly over the pre-baked crust, spreading it out with a spatula.
    - Return the baking dish to the oven and bake for an additional 20-25 minutes, or until the filling is bubbly and set.
    - Remove the pecan pie bars from the oven and let them cool completely in the pan on a wire rack.

5. Serve:

    - Once cooled, use the parchment paper overhang to lift the pecan pie bars out of the pan.
    - Place them on a cutting board and cut into squares or rectangles.
    - Serve the pecan pie bars at room temperature or slightly warmed. Optionally, you can serve them with a scoop of vanilla ice cream or a dollop of whipped cream.

Enjoy these delicious pecan pie bars as a decadent dessert or a sweet treat any time of the day!

Macadamia Nut Biscotti

Ingredients:

- 2 cups all-purpose flour
- 1 cup granulated sugar
- 1 teaspoon baking powder
- 1/4 teaspoon salt
- 1/2 cup unsalted butter, softened
- 2 large eggs
- 1 teaspoon vanilla extract
- 3/4 cup macadamia nuts, roughly chopped
- Optional: 4 ounces white chocolate, for drizzling

Instructions:

1. Preheat the Oven:

Preheat your oven to 350°F (175°C). Line a baking sheet with parchment paper or a silicone baking mat.

2. Mix Dry Ingredients:

In a mixing bowl, whisk together the flour, sugar, baking powder, and salt until well combined.

3. Cream Butter and Sugar:

In a separate bowl, cream together the softened butter and granulated sugar until light and fluffy.

4. Add Eggs and Vanilla:

Beat in the eggs, one at a time, until well incorporated. Then, mix in the vanilla extract.

5. Combine Wet and Dry Ingredients:

Gradually add the dry ingredients to the wet ingredients, mixing until a dough forms. Fold in the chopped macadamia nuts until evenly distributed.

6. Shape the Dough:

Divide the dough in half. On the prepared baking sheet, shape each half into a log about 12 inches long and 2 inches wide. Leave some space between the logs as they will spread during baking.

7. Bake:

Bake the logs in the preheated oven for 25-30 minutes, or until lightly golden and firm to the touch. Remove from the oven and let them cool on the baking sheet for 10-15 minutes.

8. Slice the Biscotti:

Using a sharp knife, slice the baked logs diagonally into 1/2-inch thick slices. Place the slices cut side down back onto the baking sheet.

9. Bake Again:

Return the biscotti slices to the oven and bake for an additional 10-12 minutes, flipping them halfway through, until they are crisp and golden brown.

10. Optional: Drizzle with White Chocolate:

If desired, melt the white chocolate in a heatproof bowl set over a pot of simmering water or in the microwave. Drizzle the melted chocolate over the cooled biscotti for an extra touch of sweetness.

11. Cool and Serve:

Let the biscotti cool completely on a wire rack before serving. Store in an airtight container at room temperature for up to two weeks.

Enjoy these delectable macadamia nut biscotti with a cup of coffee or tea for a delightful treat!

Sunflower Seed Crackers

Ingredients:

- 1 cup sunflower seeds (raw or roasted, unsalted)
- 1/4 cup flaxseed meal
- 1/4 cup sesame seeds
- 1/4 cup chia seeds
- 1/4 cup pumpkin seeds (optional)
- 1/4 cup water
- 2 tablespoons olive oil or melted coconut oil
- 1/2 teaspoon salt
- 1/2 teaspoon garlic powder (optional)
- 1/2 teaspoon onion powder (optional)
- Herbs or spices of your choice (e.g., rosemary, thyme, paprika, etc., optional)

Instructions:

Preheat the Oven:
Preheat your oven to 325°F (160°C). Line a baking sheet with parchment paper.

Prepare the Seed Mixture:
In a large mixing bowl, combine the sunflower seeds, flaxseed meal, sesame seeds, chia seeds, and pumpkin seeds (if using).

Add Flavorings:
Sprinkle the salt, garlic powder, onion powder, and any additional herbs or spices you desire over the seed mixture. Mix well to combine.

Add Liquid Ingredients:
Pour the water and olive oil (or melted coconut oil) over the seed mixture. Stir until the ingredients are evenly distributed and the mixture starts to come together. You may need to use your hands to ensure everything is well combined.

Form the Dough:
Transfer the dough onto the prepared baking sheet. Use your hands to press the dough into a thin, even layer, about 1/8 to 1/4 inch thick. You can use another sheet of parchment paper on top to help with this process and prevent sticking.

Score the Dough:

Use a knife or pizza cutter to score the dough into squares or rectangles, depending on your preference. This will make it easier to break the crackers apart once they are baked.

Bake:

Place the baking sheet in the preheated oven and bake the crackers for 25-30 minutes, or until they are golden brown and crispy around the edges.

Cool and Break Apart:

Remove the baking sheet from the oven and let the crackers cool completely. Once cooled, break them apart along the scored lines into individual crackers.

Serve or Store:

Serve the sunflower seed crackers on their own or with your favorite dips, cheeses, or spreads. Store any leftovers in an airtight container at room temperature for up to one week.

Enjoy these homemade sunflower seed crackers as a wholesome and crunchy snack anytime!

Pistachio Lemon Bars

Ingredients:

For the Crust:

- 1 cup all-purpose flour
- 1/4 cup powdered sugar
- 1/2 cup unsalted butter, softened

For the Filling:

- 4 large eggs
- 1 1/2 cups granulated sugar
- 1/2 cup lemon juice (about 4-5 lemons)
- Zest of 2 lemons
- 1/4 cup all-purpose flour
- 1/4 teaspoon baking powder
- 1/2 cup shelled pistachios, chopped
- Powdered sugar, for dusting (optional)

Instructions:

1. Preheat the Oven:

Preheat your oven to 350°F (175°C). Grease or line a 9x9-inch baking dish with parchment paper, leaving an overhang on the sides for easy removal.

2. Make the Crust:

- In a mixing bowl, combine the flour and powdered sugar.
- Cut in the softened butter using a pastry cutter or two knives until the mixture resembles coarse crumbs.
- Press the mixture evenly into the bottom of the prepared baking dish.
- Bake the crust in the preheated oven for 15-20 minutes, or until lightly golden.

3. Prepare the Filling:

- In a separate bowl, whisk together the eggs and granulated sugar until well combined.
- Add the lemon juice and lemon zest to the egg mixture, stirring until smooth.

- Sift in the flour and baking powder, and mix until incorporated.
- Fold in the chopped pistachios until evenly distributed.

4. Assemble and Bake:

- Pour the filling over the pre-baked crust, spreading it out evenly.
- Return the baking dish to the oven and bake for 25-30 minutes, or until the filling is set and the edges are lightly golden.

5. Cool and Serve:

- Remove the baking dish from the oven and let the pistachio lemon bars cool completely in the pan on a wire rack.
- Once cooled, dust the top with powdered sugar, if desired.
- Use the parchment paper overhang to lift the bars out of the pan, then transfer them to a cutting board.
- Cut the bars into squares or rectangles, and serve.

Enjoy these delectable pistachio lemon bars as a refreshing and nutty dessert or snack! They're perfect for any occasion and sure to be a crowd-pleaser.

Sesame Seed Breadsticks

Ingredients:

- 2 cups all-purpose flour
- 1 teaspoon salt
- 1 teaspoon sugar
- 1 tablespoon active dry yeast
- 3/4 cup warm water
- 2 tablespoons olive oil
- 1/4 cup sesame seeds (white or black), plus extra for sprinkling
- Coarse sea salt, for sprinkling (optional)

Instructions:

1. Prepare the Dough:

    - In a large mixing bowl, combine the warm water, sugar, and active dry yeast. Let it sit for about 5-10 minutes until the yeast activates and becomes frothy.
    - Add the flour, salt, olive oil, and sesame seeds to the yeast mixture. Stir until a dough forms.
    - Turn the dough out onto a lightly floured surface and knead for about 5-7 minutes until the dough becomes smooth and elastic.

2. Let the Dough Rise:

    - Place the dough in a greased bowl, cover it with a clean kitchen towel or plastic wrap, and let it rise in a warm place for about 1 hour, or until it doubles in size.

3. Preheat the Oven:

    - Preheat your oven to 375°F (190°C). Line a baking sheet with parchment paper.

4. Shape the Breadsticks:

    - Punch down the risen dough to deflate it. Divide the dough into equal-sized portions, depending on how large you want your breadsticks to be.
    - Roll each portion of dough into a long rope, about 1/2 inch in diameter. If the dough is sticky, lightly dust your hands and the work surface with flour.

5. Add Sesame Seeds:

    - Spread some sesame seeds on a plate. Roll each breadstick in the sesame seeds, coating them evenly.

6. Bake:
    - Place the sesame seed-coated breadsticks on the prepared baking sheet, leaving space between each stick.
    - If desired, sprinkle the breadsticks lightly with coarse sea salt for extra flavor.
    - Bake in the preheated oven for 12-15 minutes, or until the breadsticks are golden brown and crispy.

7. Cool and Serve:
    - Remove the baking sheet from the oven and let the breadsticks cool for a few minutes before transferring them to a wire rack to cool completely.
    - Once cooled, serve the sesame seed breadsticks with your favorite dips, spreads, or enjoy them on their own as a crunchy snack.

These sesame seed breadsticks are best enjoyed fresh but can be stored in an airtight container for a few days. Enjoy the crunchy goodness!

Pine Nut Energy Balls

Ingredients:

- 1 cup pitted dates
- 1 cup raw almonds
- 1/2 cup pine nuts
- 2 tablespoons unsweetened cocoa powder
- 1 tablespoon honey or maple syrup (optional, for added sweetness)
- 1 teaspoon vanilla extract
- Pinch of salt
- Desiccated coconut or additional pine nuts for coating (optional)

Instructions:

Prepare the Ingredients:
- If your dates are not soft, soak them in warm water for about 10 minutes, then drain.
- Toast the pine nuts in a dry skillet over medium heat for a few minutes until lightly golden and fragrant. Allow them to cool.

Blend Ingredients:
- In a food processor, combine the dates, almonds, toasted pine nuts, cocoa powder, honey or maple syrup (if using), vanilla extract, and a pinch of salt.
- Pulse the ingredients until they are finely chopped and start to come together into a sticky dough. Scrape down the sides of the food processor as needed.

Form Balls:
- Take small portions of the mixture and roll it between your palms to form small balls. If the mixture is too sticky, dampen your hands slightly with water.

Coat (Optional):
- Roll the energy balls in desiccated coconut or additional pine nuts to coat them, if desired. This step adds extra flavor and texture.

Chill:
- Place the energy balls on a baking sheet lined with parchment paper and refrigerate them for at least 30 minutes to firm up.

Store or Serve:
- Once chilled, the pine nut energy balls are ready to eat. Enjoy them as a quick snack or whenever you need a burst of energy.

- Store any leftover energy balls in an airtight container in the refrigerator for up to two weeks, or freeze them for longer storage.

These pine nut energy balls are not only delicious but also packed with nutrients and natural energy sources, making them a perfect snack for on-the-go or pre/post-workout fuel.

Brazil Nut Fudge

Ingredients:

- 2 cups Brazil nuts, chopped
- 1 can (14 ounces) sweetened condensed milk
- 1/2 cup unsalted butter
- 1 teaspoon vanilla extract
- Pinch of salt
- Optional: Additional chopped Brazil nuts for topping

Instructions:

Prepare the Pan:
- Line an 8x8 inch baking dish with parchment paper, leaving some overhang on the sides for easy removal later. Alternatively, grease the dish lightly with butter.

Toast the Brazil Nuts (Optional):
- If desired, toast the chopped Brazil nuts in a dry skillet over medium heat for a few minutes until fragrant. This step enhances their flavor, but it's optional.

Melt Ingredients:
- In a medium saucepan, combine the sweetened condensed milk, unsalted butter, and pinch of salt over medium heat.
- Cook, stirring constantly, until the mixture is smooth and well combined.

Add Flavorings:
- Stir in the vanilla extract and the chopped Brazil nuts until evenly distributed throughout the mixture.

Cook Until Thickened:
- Continue to cook the mixture, stirring constantly, until it thickens and starts to pull away from the sides of the pan. This usually takes about 5-7 minutes.

Pour into Pan:
- Once the mixture has thickened, quickly pour it into the prepared baking dish, spreading it out evenly with a spatula.

Optional Topping:
- If desired, sprinkle additional chopped Brazil nuts on top of the fudge and gently press them into the surface.

Chill:

- Place the pan of fudge in the refrigerator and let it chill for at least 2 hours, or until firm.

Slice and Serve:
- Once the fudge is firm, use the parchment paper overhang to lift it out of the pan. Place it on a cutting board and slice it into squares or bars.
- Serve the Brazil nut fudge at room temperature and enjoy!

Storage:
- Store any leftover fudge in an airtight container in the refrigerator for up to one week.

This Brazil nut fudge makes a delicious treat for any occasion, and its creamy texture and nutty flavor are sure to be a hit with family and friends.

Pumpkin Seed Bread

Ingredients:

- 2 cups bread flour
- 1 cup whole wheat flour
- 1 packet (2 1/4 teaspoons) active dry yeast
- 1 teaspoon salt
- 1 tablespoon honey or maple syrup
- 1 cup warm water (110°F to 115°F)
- 1/4 cup pumpkin puree (canned or homemade)
- 1/4 cup pumpkin seeds (plus extra for topping)
- 2 tablespoons olive oil

Instructions:

Activate Yeast:
- In a small bowl, combine the warm water, honey (or maple syrup), and yeast. Stir gently to dissolve the yeast. Let it sit for about 5-10 minutes until the mixture becomes frothy, indicating that the yeast is activated.

Mix Dry Ingredients:
- In a large mixing bowl, combine the bread flour, whole wheat flour, and salt.

Combine Wet Ingredients:
- In a separate bowl, mix together the pumpkin puree and olive oil.

Make Dough:
- Add the activated yeast mixture to the dry ingredients, along with the pumpkin puree mixture. Stir until a rough dough forms.
- Turn the dough out onto a lightly floured surface and knead for about 8-10 minutes until the dough is smooth and elastic. Alternatively, you can use a stand mixer with a dough hook attachment to knead the dough.

Incorporate Pumpkin Seeds:
- Knead in the pumpkin seeds until they are evenly distributed throughout the dough.

First Rise:
- Place the dough in a greased bowl, cover it with a clean kitchen towel or plastic wrap, and let it rise in a warm place for about 1-2 hours, or until it doubles in size.

Shape the Dough:

- Punch down the risen dough to deflate it. Shape it into a loaf and place it in a greased loaf pan. Alternatively, you can shape the dough into a round or oval loaf and place it on a greased baking sheet.

Second Rise:
- Cover the shaped dough with a clean kitchen towel or plastic wrap and let it rise for another 30-45 minutes, or until it slightly rises above the rim of the loaf pan or spreads out on the baking sheet.

Preheat the Oven:
- While the dough is rising, preheat your oven to 375°F (190°C).

Add Pumpkin Seed Topping:
- If desired, sprinkle some additional pumpkin seeds on top of the loaf before baking for added decoration and flavor.

Bake:
- Bake the pumpkin seed bread in the preheated oven for 30-35 minutes (for a loaf) or 25-30 minutes (for a free-form loaf), or until the bread is golden brown and sounds hollow when tapped on the bottom.

Cool and Serve:
- Remove the bread from the oven and let it cool in the pan for a few minutes before transferring it to a wire rack to cool completely.
- Slice and serve the pumpkin seed bread warm or at room temperature. Enjoy with butter, jam, or your favorite toppings.

This homemade pumpkin seed bread is perfect for sandwiches, toast, or enjoying on its own as a delicious and nutritious snack.

Almond Joy Bites

Ingredients:

- 1 cup shredded coconut (sweetened or unsweetened)
- 1/2 cup almond flour
- 1/4 cup maple syrup or honey
- 2 tablespoons coconut oil, melted
- 1 teaspoon vanilla extract
- Pinch of salt
- 24 whole almonds
- 4 ounces dark chocolate (or milk chocolate), chopped
- 1 tablespoon coconut oil

Instructions:

Prepare the Coconut Mixture:
- In a mixing bowl, combine the shredded coconut, almond flour, maple syrup (or honey), melted coconut oil, vanilla extract, and a pinch of salt. Mix until well combined and the mixture holds together when pressed.

Shape the Bites:
- Take small portions of the coconut mixture and roll them into balls about 1 inch in diameter. Press an almond into the center of each ball, flattening slightly to resemble the shape of an almond joy candy.

Chill:
- Place the shaped almond joy bites on a baking sheet lined with parchment paper and chill them in the refrigerator for about 30 minutes to firm up.

Prepare the Chocolate Coating:
- In a heatproof bowl set over a pot of simmering water (or in the microwave), melt the chopped chocolate and tablespoon of coconut oil together, stirring until smooth and well combined.

Coat the Bites:
- Remove the chilled almond joy bites from the refrigerator. Using a fork or dipping tool, dip each bite into the melted chocolate until fully coated, allowing any excess chocolate to drip off.

Set:
- Place the coated bites back on the parchment-lined baking sheet. If desired, sprinkle some additional shredded coconut on top of each bite for decoration.

Chill Again:

- Return the baking sheet to the refrigerator and let the chocolate coating set for about 30 minutes to 1 hour, or until firm.

Serve or Store:
- Once the chocolate has set, the almond joy bites are ready to be enjoyed! Serve them as a delicious snack or dessert.
- Store any leftovers in an airtight container in the refrigerator for up to one week.

These homemade almond joy bites are a perfect indulgence for anyone who loves the combination of chocolate, almonds, and coconut. Enjoy their sweet and nutty flavors any time you need a little treat!

Walnut Flour Waffles

Ingredients:

- 2 cups walnut flour
- 4 large eggs
- 1/4 cup milk or almond milk
- 2 tablespoons melted butter or coconut oil
- 2 tablespoons honey or maple syrup (optional, for sweetness)
- 1 teaspoon baking powder
- 1/2 teaspoon vanilla extract
- Pinch of salt

Instructions:

Preheat the Waffle Iron:
- Preheat your waffle iron according to the manufacturer's instructions.

Prepare the Batter:
- In a large mixing bowl, whisk together the walnut flour, baking powder, and salt until well combined.
- In a separate bowl, beat the eggs and then mix in the milk, melted butter (or coconut oil), honey (or maple syrup), and vanilla extract until smooth.

Combine Wet and Dry Ingredients:
- Pour the wet ingredients into the bowl with the dry ingredients and stir until just combined. Be careful not to overmix; a few lumps are okay.

Cook the Waffles:
- Lightly grease the waffle iron with butter or cooking spray, if needed.
- Pour enough batter onto the preheated waffle iron to cover the grids. The amount will depend on the size of your waffle iron.
- Close the lid and cook the waffles according to the manufacturer's instructions, typically about 3-5 minutes, or until golden brown and crispy.

Serve:
- Once cooked, carefully remove the waffles from the waffle iron and serve them immediately.
- Optionally, top the walnut flour waffles with your favorite toppings such as fresh fruit, yogurt, maple syrup, or a dusting of powdered sugar.

Storage:
- If you have leftover waffles, allow them to cool completely before storing them in an airtight container in the refrigerator for up to 3 days. You can

also freeze them for longer storage. Reheat in a toaster or toaster oven before serving.

Enjoy these delicious and nutritious walnut flour waffles for breakfast, brunch, or any time you're craving a tasty waffle treat!

Cashew Cream Frosting

Ingredients:

- 1 cup raw cashews, soaked in water for at least 4 hours or overnight
- 1/4 cup coconut cream or full-fat coconut milk
- 1/4 cup maple syrup or agave syrup (adjust to taste)
- 1 tablespoon lemon juice
- 1 teaspoon vanilla extract
- Pinch of salt
- Optional: additional sweetener to taste

Instructions:

Soak Cashews:
- Place the raw cashews in a bowl and cover them with water. Let them soak for at least 4 hours or overnight. Soaking softens the cashews, making them easier to blend and resulting in a creamier texture.

Drain and Rinse:
- After soaking, drain and rinse the cashews thoroughly under cold water.

Blend:
- In a blender or food processor, combine the soaked and drained cashews, coconut cream or coconut milk, maple syrup or agave syrup, lemon juice, vanilla extract, and a pinch of salt.
- Blend on high speed until the mixture is smooth and creamy. You may need to stop and scrape down the sides of the blender or food processor a few times to ensure even blending.

Taste and Adjust:
- Taste the cashew cream frosting and adjust the sweetness or acidity to your liking. Add more maple syrup or lemon juice if desired.

Chill (Optional):
- If the frosting is too thin, you can chill it in the refrigerator for about 30 minutes to firm up slightly before using. However, if you prefer a softer consistency, you can use it right away.

Frosting:
- Once the cashew cream frosting reaches the desired consistency, use it to frost cakes, cupcakes, or other desserts. Spread it evenly over the surface using an offset spatula or piping bag, as desired.

Serve or Store:

- Serve the frosted desserts immediately, or store them in the refrigerator until ready to serve.
- Any leftover cashew cream frosting can be stored in an airtight container in the refrigerator for up to 5 days. Give it a stir before using it again.

Enjoy this delicious and creamy cashew cream frosting on your favorite baked treats!

It's perfect for anyone looking for a dairy-free and vegan frosting option.

Coconut Macaroons

Ingredients:

- 3 cups shredded coconut (sweetened or unsweetened, depending on preference)
- 1 can (14 ounces) sweetened condensed milk
- 2 teaspoons vanilla extract
- 2 large egg whites
- 1/4 teaspoon salt
- Optional: melted chocolate for dipping or drizzling (dark, milk, or white chocolate)

Instructions:

Preheat the Oven:
- Preheat your oven to 325°F (160°C). Line a baking sheet with parchment paper or a silicone baking mat.

Mix Ingredients:
- In a large mixing bowl, combine the shredded coconut, sweetened condensed milk, and vanilla extract. Stir until well combined.

Whip Egg Whites:
- In a separate bowl, beat the egg whites and salt until stiff peaks form. This will help give the macaroons their light and airy texture.

Fold in Egg Whites:
- Gently fold the whipped egg whites into the coconut mixture until evenly incorporated. Be careful not to deflate the egg whites too much.

Form Macaroons:
- Using a spoon or cookie scoop, drop rounded tablespoons of the coconut mixture onto the prepared baking sheet, spacing them about 1 inch apart. You can also shape them into small mounds using your hands if preferred.

Bake:
- Bake the macaroons in the preheated oven for 15-20 minutes, or until the edges are golden brown and the tops are lightly toasted.

Cool:
- Remove the baking sheet from the oven and let the macaroons cool on the pan for a few minutes before transferring them to a wire rack to cool completely.

Optional Chocolate Dip:
- If desired, melt chocolate (dark, milk, or white) in a heatproof bowl set over a pot of simmering water or in the microwave. Dip the bottoms of the

cooled macaroons into the melted chocolate, or drizzle the chocolate over the tops for added flavor and decoration.

Set Chocolate:
- Place the chocolate-dipped or drizzled macaroons on parchment paper and let them sit at room temperature until the chocolate sets.

Serve or Store:
- Once the chocolate has set, the coconut macaroons are ready to be enjoyed! Serve them as a delicious treat or store them in an airtight container at room temperature for up to one week.

These coconut macaroons are simple to make and perfect for satisfying your sweet tooth. Enjoy their chewy texture and coconut flavor with or without a chocolatey finish!

Hazelnut Chocolate Spread

Ingredients:

- 1 1/2 cups raw hazelnuts
- 1 cup semi-sweet chocolate chips or chopped chocolate (adjust according to your preference)
- 1/4 cup cocoa powder
- 1/2 cup powdered sugar (adjust according to sweetness preference)
- 1/4 teaspoon salt
- 2-4 tablespoons hazelnut oil or vegetable oil (adjust for desired consistency)
- 1 teaspoon vanilla extract (optional)

Instructions:

Roast the Hazelnuts:
- Preheat your oven to 350°F (175°C). Spread the hazelnuts in a single layer on a baking sheet.
- Roast the hazelnuts in the preheated oven for about 10-12 minutes, or until they are fragrant and the skins are starting to crack.

Remove Skins:
- Once roasted, transfer the hazelnuts to a clean kitchen towel. Fold the towel over the hazelnuts and rub them vigorously to remove as much of the skins as possible.

Prepare Hazelnut Paste:
- In a food processor, grind the roasted hazelnuts until they form a smooth, creamy hazelnut paste. This process may take a few minutes, and you may need to scrape down the sides of the food processor occasionally.

Melt Chocolate:
- In a microwave-safe bowl or double boiler, melt the chocolate chips or chopped chocolate until smooth and completely melted.

Combine Ingredients:
- Add the melted chocolate, cocoa powder, powdered sugar, salt, and vanilla extract (if using) to the hazelnut paste in the food processor.

Blend:
- Blend all the ingredients together in the food processor until smooth and well combined. While blending, drizzle in the hazelnut oil or vegetable oil gradually until you reach your desired consistency. The oil helps to loosen the spread and make it smoother.

Adjust Sweetness and Texture:

- Taste the hazelnut chocolate spread and adjust the sweetness and texture according to your preference. You can add more powdered sugar for sweetness or more oil for a smoother consistency.

Store:
- Transfer the hazelnut chocolate spread to a clean jar or airtight container. It can be stored at room temperature for a few days or in the refrigerator for longer shelf life.

Enjoy:
- Spread the homemade hazelnut chocolate spread on toast, pancakes, waffles, or use it as a dip for fruits or crackers. It's also perfect for making desserts or adding to baked goods.

This homemade hazelnut chocolate spread is rich, creamy, and full of nutty chocolate flavor. Enjoy it on its own or use it as a delicious topping or filling for your favorite treats!

Pecan Butter Cookies

Ingredients:

- 1 cup unsalted butter, softened
- 1 cup pecan halves, finely chopped
- 1 cup powdered sugar
- 2 cups all-purpose flour
- 1 teaspoon vanilla extract
- 1/4 teaspoon salt

Instructions:

Preheat the oven: Preheat your oven to 350°F (175°C). Line a baking sheet with parchment paper or lightly grease it.

Toast the pecans: Spread the pecan halves on a baking sheet and toast them in the preheated oven for about 8-10 minutes, or until fragrant. Keep an eye on them to prevent burning. Once toasted, remove them from the oven and let them cool. Then, finely chop them.

Cream butter and sugar: In a mixing bowl, cream together the softened butter and powdered sugar until light and fluffy.

Add vanilla: Mix in the vanilla extract until well combined.

Incorporate dry ingredients: Gradually add the flour and salt to the butter mixture, mixing until a dough forms.

Fold in pecans: Gently fold in the chopped pecans until evenly distributed throughout the dough.

Shape the cookies: Roll the dough into small balls, about 1 inch in diameter, and place them on the prepared baking sheet. Flatten each ball slightly with the back of a fork or your fingers.

Bake: Bake the cookies in the preheated oven for 12-15 minutes, or until the edges are golden brown.

Cool and serve: Allow the cookies to cool on the baking sheet for a few minutes before transferring them to a wire rack to cool completely.

Enjoy: Once cooled, serve and enjoy these delicious pecan butter cookies with a glass of milk or your favorite hot beverage.

These cookies can be stored in an airtight container at room temperature for several days. Enjoy!

Macadamia Nut Granola

Ingredients:

- 3 cups old-fashioned rolled oats
- 1 cup chopped macadamia nuts
- 1/2 cup shredded coconut (unsweetened)
- 1/4 cup honey or maple syrup
- 1/4 cup coconut oil, melted
- 1 teaspoon vanilla extract
- 1/2 teaspoon ground cinnamon
- 1/4 teaspoon salt
- Optional: 1/2 cup dried fruit (such as chopped dried pineapple or dried cranberries)

Instructions:

Preheat the oven: Preheat your oven to 300°F (150°C). Line a baking sheet with parchment paper or a silicone baking mat.

Mix dry ingredients: In a large mixing bowl, combine the rolled oats, chopped macadamia nuts, shredded coconut, ground cinnamon, and salt. Mix well to combine.

Add wet ingredients: In a separate bowl, whisk together the honey or maple syrup, melted coconut oil, and vanilla extract until smooth.

Combine wet and dry ingredients: Pour the wet mixture over the dry ingredients in the large mixing bowl. Stir until all the dry ingredients are evenly coated with the wet mixture.

Spread on baking sheet: Spread the granola mixture evenly onto the prepared baking sheet in a single layer.

Bake: Bake the granola in the preheated oven for 25-30 minutes, stirring halfway through, or until golden brown and fragrant.

Add dried fruit (optional): If using dried fruit, add it to the granola immediately after removing it from the oven. Stir to combine.

Cool: Allow the granola to cool completely on the baking sheet. It will crisp up as it cools.

Store: Once cooled, transfer the granola to an airtight container or resealable bag for storage. It will keep for several weeks at room temperature.

Serve and enjoy: Serve the macadamia nut granola with milk or yogurt for breakfast, or enjoy it as a snack on its own.

Feel free to customize this recipe by adding other nuts, seeds, or spices to suit your taste preferences. Enjoy your homemade macadamia nut granola!

Sunflower Seed Bread

Ingredients:

- 2 cups whole wheat flour
- 1 cup all-purpose flour
- 1/2 cup sunflower seeds (plus extra for topping)
- 2 tablespoons honey or maple syrup
- 2 tablespoons olive oil or melted butter
- 1 1/4 cups warm water (about 110°F/45°C)
- 1 packet (2 1/4 teaspoons) active dry yeast
- 1 teaspoon salt

Instructions:

Activate the yeast: In a small bowl, combine the warm water and honey or maple syrup. Sprinkle the yeast over the mixture and let it sit for about 5-10 minutes, until foamy.
Mix the dough: In a large mixing bowl, combine the whole wheat flour, all-purpose flour, sunflower seeds, and salt. Make a well in the center and pour in the activated yeast mixture and olive oil or melted butter.
Knead the dough: Using a wooden spoon or your hands, mix until a dough forms. Turn the dough out onto a floured surface and knead for about 8-10 minutes, until smooth and elastic.
First rise: Place the dough in a lightly oiled bowl, cover with a clean kitchen towel or plastic wrap, and let it rise in a warm, draft-free place for about 1-1.5 hours, or until doubled in size.
Shape the loaf: Punch down the risen dough and shape it into a loaf. Place it in a greased or parchment-lined loaf pan. Optionally, sprinkle extra sunflower seeds on top of the loaf.
Second rise: Cover the loaf pan with a clean kitchen towel or plastic wrap and let the dough rise for another 30-45 minutes, until it rises slightly above the rim of the pan.
Preheat the oven: Preheat your oven to 375°F (190°C) while the dough is undergoing its second rise.
Bake: Once the dough has risen, bake the bread in the preheated oven for 30-35 minutes, or until golden brown and hollow-sounding when tapped on the bottom.
Cool and slice: Remove the bread from the oven and let it cool in the pan for a few minutes beore transferring it to a wire rack to cool completely. Slice and serve.

Enjoy your homemade sunflower seed bread with your favorite spreads or as a complement to soups and salads!

Pistachio Rosewater Cake

Ingredients:

For the Cake:

- 1 cup shelled pistachios
- 1 cup all-purpose flour
- 1 teaspoon baking powder
- 1/4 teaspoon salt
- 1/2 cup unsalted butter, softened
- 1 cup granulated sugar
- 3 large eggs
- 1/2 cup milk
- 1 teaspoon pure vanilla extract
- 1-2 tablespoons rosewater (adjust to taste)

For the Frosting:

- 1/2 cup unsalted butter, softened
- 2 cups powdered sugar
- 1-2 tablespoons rosewater
- A few drops of pink food coloring (optional)
- Chopped pistachios for garnish (optional)

Instructions:

Preheat your oven to 350°F (175°C). Grease and flour a 9-inch round cake pan or line it with parchment paper.
In a food processor, pulse the pistachios until finely ground. Be careful not to over-process, or they'll turn into pistachio butter.
In a medium bowl, whisk together the ground pistachios, flour, baking powder, and salt. Set aside.
In a large mixing bowl, cream together the softened butter and sugar until light and fluffy.
Add the eggs, one at a time, beating well after each addition. Mix in the vanilla extract.
Gradually add the dry ingredients to the wet ingredients, alternating with the milk, beginning and ending with the dry ingredients. Mix until just combined.
Stir in the rosewater to the batter, adjusting the amount to your preference. Start with 1 tablespoon and taste, adding more if desired.
Pour the batter into the prepared cake pan and smooth the top with a spatula.
Bake in the preheated oven for 25-30 minutes, or until a toothpick inserted into the center of the cake comes out clean.
Allow the cake to cool in the pan for 10 minutes before transferring it to a wire rack to cool completely.

While the cake is cooling, prepare the frosting. In a mixing bowl, beat together the softened butter, powdered sugar, and rosewater until smooth and creamy. Add a few drops of pink food coloring if desired.

Once the cake is completely cooled, frost the top and sides with the prepared frosting. Garnish the cake with chopped pistachios if desired.

Slice and serve your Pistachio Rosewater Cake and enjoy!

This cake is perfect for special occasions or as a sweet treat for any day. The combination of pistachio and rosewater creates a unique and delightful flavor that will impress your friends and family.

Sesame Seed Cookies

Ingredients:

- 1 cup all-purpose flour
- 1/2 teaspoon baking powder
- 1/4 teaspoon salt
- 1/2 cup unsalted butter, softened
- 1/2 cup granulated sugar
- 1 large egg
- 1 teaspoon vanilla extract
- 1/2 cup sesame seeds

Instructions:

Preheat your oven to 350°F (175°C). Line a baking sheet with parchment paper or lightly grease it.
In a small bowl, whisk together the flour, baking powder, and salt. Set aside.
In a large mixing bowl, cream together the softened butter and sugar until light and fluffy.
Beat in the egg and vanilla extract until well combined.
Gradually add the dry ingredients to the wet ingredients, mixing until a dough forms.
Spread the sesame seeds out on a plate.
Take about a tablespoon of dough and roll it into a ball between your palms. Then roll the dough ball in the sesame seeds, coating it evenly.
Place the coated dough ball onto the prepared baking sheet and gently flatten it with the palm of your hand or the bottom of a glass. Leave some space between each cookie as they will spread slightly during baking.
Repeat the process with the remaining dough, rolling each ball in sesame seeds and placing them on the baking sheet.
Bake the cookies in the preheated oven for 10-12 minutes, or until the edges are lightly golden brown.
Allow the cookies to cool on the baking sheet for a few minutes before transferring them to a wire rack to cool completely.
Once cooled, serve and enjoy your delicious sesame seed cookies!

These cookies are perfect for enjoying with a cup of tea or coffee, or as a snack any time of the day. The sesame seeds add a wonderful nutty flavor and texture, making them a unique and tasty treat.

Brazil Nut Truffles

Ingredients:

- 1 cup Brazil nuts
- 1 cup pitted dates
- 2 tablespoons cocoa powder
- 1 teaspoon vanilla extract
- Pinch of salt
- Desiccated coconut or cocoa powder for coating (optional)

Instructions:

In a food processor, pulse the Brazil nuts until finely chopped.
Add the pitted dates, cocoa powder, vanilla extract, and a pinch of salt to the food processor with the chopped Brazil nuts.
Process the mixture until it forms a thick and sticky dough. If the mixture is too dry, you can add a few drops of water or a teaspoon of coconut oil to help bind it together.
Once the mixture has formed a dough-like consistency, scoop out tablespoon-sized portions and roll them into balls between your palms. If desired, you can roll the balls in desiccated coconut or cocoa powder for an extra layer of flavor and texture.
Place the rolled truffles on a baking sheet lined with parchment paper and chill them in the refrigerator for at least 30 minutes to firm up.
Once chilled, your Brazil nut truffles are ready to serve. Enjoy them as a delicious snack or dessert!

These truffles are not only decadently delicious but also naturally sweetened with dates and packed with the rich flavor of Brazil nuts. They make a perfect healthier alternative to traditional truffles and are sure to satisfy your sweet cravings.

Pumpkin Seed Crackers

Ingredients:

- 1 cup pumpkin seeds (raw or toasted)
- 1/4 cup ground flaxseed
- 1/4 cup sesame seeds
- 1/4 cup sunflower seeds
- 1/4 cup chia seeds
- 1/4 cup water
- 1/2 teaspoon salt
- 1/2 teaspoon garlic powder (optional)
- 1/2 teaspoon onion powder (optional)
- 1/4 teaspoon black pepper (optional)
- Other optional seasonings such as paprika, cumin, or rosemary

Instructions:

Preheat your oven to 325°F (160°C). Line a baking sheet with parchment paper or a silicone baking mat.
In a large bowl, combine the pumpkin seeds, ground flaxseed, sesame seeds, sunflower seeds, and chia seeds.
In a separate small bowl, mix together the water, salt, and any optional seasonings you desire, such as garlic powder, onion powder, black pepper, or other herbs and spices.
Pour the wet ingredients over the seed mixture and stir until everything is well combined and evenly coated. The mixture should be slightly sticky and hold together when pressed.
Transfer the mixture onto the prepared baking sheet and spread it out evenly.
Place another sheet of parchment paper on top of the mixture and use a rolling pin to roll it out into a thin, even layer, about 1/8 to 1/4 inch thick.
Remove the top sheet of parchment paper and use a sharp knife or pizza cutter to score the dough into desired cracker shapes. You can make squares, rectangles, or triangles.
Bake the crackers in the preheated oven for 20-25 minutes, or until they are golden brown and crispy. Keep an eye on them towards the end of the baking time to prevent burning.
Once the crackers are done baking, remove them from the oven and allow them to cool completely on the baking sheet. They will continue to crisp up as they cool.

Once cooled, break the crackers apart along the scored lines and store them in an airtight container at room temperature for up to 1 week.

Enjoy your homemade pumpkin seed crackers as a nutritious snack on their own or paired with your favorite dips, spreads, or cheeses. They're perfect for snacking, entertaining, or adding a crunchy topping to salads and soups.

Almond Flour Biscuits

Ingredients:

- 2 cups almond flour
- 1/4 cup coconut flour
- 2 teaspoons baking powder
- 1/2 teaspoon salt
- 1/4 cup unsalted butter, cold and cubed
- 2 large eggs
- 1/4 cup unsweetened almond milk or any milk of your choice

Instructions:

Preheat your oven to 350°F (175°C). Line a baking sheet with parchment paper or lightly grease it.

In a large mixing bowl, whisk together the almond flour, coconut flour, baking powder, and salt until well combined.

Add the cold cubed butter to the dry ingredients. Using a pastry cutter or your fingers, work the butter into the flour mixture until it resembles coarse crumbs.

In a separate small bowl, whisk together the eggs and almond milk until well combined.

Pour the wet ingredients into the dry ingredients and mix until a dough forms. The dough should be slightly sticky but manageable. If it's too dry, you can add a little more almond milk, 1 tablespoon at a time, until you reach the desired consistency.

Turn the dough out onto a lightly almond-floured surface. Gently knead it a few times until it comes together.

Pat or roll the dough out to about 1/2 to 3/4 inch thickness.

Use a biscuit cutter or a glass to cut out biscuits from the dough. Press straight down and lift straight up without twisting to ensure the biscuits rise evenly.

Place the biscuits onto the prepared baking sheet, leaving a little space between each one.

Gather any remaining dough scraps, gently pat them together, and cut out more biscuits until all the dough is used.

Bake the biscuits in the preheated oven for 12-15 minutes, or until they are golden brown on top and cooked through.

Remove the biscuits from the oven and let them cool slightly on the baking sheet before transferring them to a wire rack to cool completely.

Serve the almond flour biscuits warm with butter, jam, gravy, or your favorite toppings.

These almond flour biscuits are tender, flaky, and full of flavor. They're perfect for breakfast, brunch, or as a side dish for any meal. Enjoy!

Walnut Date Bars

Ingredients:

- 1 cup pitted dates
- 1 cup walnuts
- 1/2 cup rolled oats
- 1/4 cup shredded coconut (optional)
- 1/4 cup almond butter or peanut butter
- 1 tablespoon honey or maple syrup (optional, for added sweetness)
- Pinch of salt
- 1/2 teaspoon vanilla extract
- Additional shredded coconut or chopped walnuts for garnish (optional)

Instructions:

Preheat your oven to 350°F (175°C). Line an 8x8 inch baking pan with parchment paper, leaving some overhang on the sides for easy removal.
In a food processor, combine the pitted dates, walnuts, rolled oats, shredded coconut (if using), almond butter or peanut butter, honey or maple syrup (if using), salt, and vanilla extract.
Pulse the ingredients until they are well combined and form a sticky, crumbly mixture. The mixture should hold together when pressed between your fingers.
Transfer the mixture to the prepared baking pan and press it evenly into the bottom using the back of a spoon or your fingertips. Make sure to press firmly to compact the mixture.
If desired, sprinkle some additional shredded coconut or chopped walnuts on top of the mixture for garnish.
Bake the walnut date bars in the preheated oven for 15-20 minutes, or until the edges are golden brown.
Remove the baking pan from the oven and let the bars cool completely in the pan on a wire rack.
Once cooled, use the parchment paper overhang to lift the bars out of the pan. Place them on a cutting board and cut into squares or bars using a sharp knife.
Serve and enjoy your homemade walnut date bars! Store any leftovers in an airtight container at room temperature for up to one week.

These walnut date bars are perfect for a quick and healthy snack on the go, or as a sweet treat for any time of day. They're naturally sweetened, gluten-free, and packed with wholesome ingredients.

Cashew Cheesecake

Ingredients:

For the Crust:

- 1 1/2 cups graham cracker crumbs (or crushed cookies of your choice)
- 1/4 cup melted butter (or melted coconut oil for a vegan option)
- 2 tablespoons granulated sugar (optional)

For the Filling:

- 2 cups raw cashews, soaked in water for at least 4 hours or overnight
- 1/2 cup full-fat coconut milk
- 1/2 cup lemon juice
- 1/2 cup maple syrup (or sweetener of your choice, adjust to taste)
- 1/2 cup melted coconut oil
- 1 teaspoon vanilla extract
- Pinch of salt

Instructions:

For the Crust:

Preheat your oven to 350°F (175°C). Grease a 9-inch springform pan or line it with parchment paper.
In a mixing bowl, combine the graham cracker crumbs, melted butter, and granulated sugar (if using). Mix until well combined and the mixture resembles wet sand.
Press the crumb mixture evenly into the bottom of the prepared springform pan.
Bake the crust in the preheated oven for 10-12 minutes, or until lightly golden brown.
Remove from the oven and let it cool while you prepare the filling.

For the Filling:

Drain the soaked cashews and rinse them thoroughly under cold water.
In a high-powered blender or food processor, combine the soaked cashews, coconut milk, lemon juice, maple syrup, melted coconut oil, vanilla extract, and a pinch of salt.
Blend the mixture on high speed until smooth and creamy, scraping down the sides of the blender or food processor as needed.
Once the filling is smooth and creamy, taste and adjust the sweetness or lemon flavor as desired.
Pour the filling over the cooled crust in the springform pan, smoothing the top with a spatula.

Tap the pan gently on the counter to release any air bubbles, then cover the pan with plastic wrap or aluminum foil.

Place the cheesecake in the freezer to set for at least 4-6 hours, or preferably overnight.

Before serving, let the cheesecake thaw for 10-15 minutes at room temperature. You can also run a knife around the edges of the cheesecake to loosen it from the pan before removing the springform ring.

Slice the cashew cheesecake into wedges and serve chilled. You can garnish with fresh fruit, a drizzle of caramel or chocolate sauce, or a dollop of whipped coconut cream, if desired.

Enjoy this creamy and indulgent cashew cheesecake as a delightful dessert that's vegan-friendly and full of flavor!

Coconut Flour Tortillas

Ingredients:

- 1 cup coconut flour
- 4 large eggs
- 1/2 cup warm water
- 2 tablespoons olive oil or melted coconut oil
- 1/2 teaspoon salt

Instructions:

In a mixing bowl, whisk together the coconut flour and salt until well combined.
In a separate bowl, beat the eggs. Then add the warm water and olive oil (or melted coconut oil) to the eggs and mix until combined.
Pour the wet ingredients into the dry ingredients and mix until a smooth batter forms. If the batter is too thick, you can add a little more warm water, one tablespoon at a time, until you reach the desired consistency.
Let the batter sit for a few minutes to allow the coconut flour to absorb the liquid.
Heat a non-stick skillet or frying pan over medium heat. Lightly grease the skillet with olive oil or coconut oil.
Pour about 1/4 cup of the batter onto the skillet and use the back of a spoon to spread it out into a thin, even circle.
Cook the tortilla for 1-2 minutes on one side, or until the edges start to lift and the bottom is lightly golden brown. Flip the tortilla and cook for an additional 1-2 minutes on the other side, until cooked through.
Repeat the process with the remaining batter, greasing the skillet as needed between each tortilla.
Once cooked, transfer the tortillas to a plate and cover them with a clean kitchen towel to keep them warm.
Serve the coconut flour tortillas warm with your favorite fillings, such as grilled vegetables, chicken, beef, beans, salsa, guacamole, or cheese.

These coconut flour tortillas are soft, pliable, and perfect for wrapping up your favorite ingredients. They're also gluten-free and paleo-friendly, making them a great option for those with dietary restrictions. Enjoy!

Pecan Crumble Apple Pie

Ingredients:

For the Pie Crust:

- 1 1/4 cups all-purpose flour
- 1/2 teaspoon salt
- 1/2 cup unsalted butter, cold and cubed
- 3-4 tablespoons ice water

For the Apple Filling:

- 6 cups peeled and thinly sliced apples (such as Granny Smith or Honeycrisp)
- 1/2 cup granulated sugar
- 1/4 cup packed light brown sugar
- 2 tablespoons all-purpose flour
- 1 teaspoon ground cinnamon
- 1/4 teaspoon ground nutmeg
- 1 tablespoon lemon juice

For the Pecan Crumble Topping:

- 1/2 cup all-purpose flour
- 1/2 cup packed light brown sugar
- 1/2 cup chopped pecans
- 1/4 cup unsalted butter, melted

Instructions:

For the Pie Crust:

In a large mixing bowl, combine the flour and salt. Add the cold cubed butter and use a pastry cutter or fork to cut the butter into the flour mixture until it resembles coarse crumbs.
Gradually add the ice water, one tablespoon at a time, and mix until the dough comes together. Be careful not to overwork the dough.
Shape the dough into a disk, wrap it in plastic wrap, and refrigerate it for at least 30 minutes.
Preheat your oven to 375°F (190°C).

On a lightly floured surface, roll out the chilled pie crust into a circle about 12 inches in diameter. Carefully transfer the dough to a 9-inch pie dish and trim any excess dough from the edges. Crimp the edges with a fork or your fingers. Place the pie crust in the refrigerator while you prepare the filling and topping.

For the Apple Filling:

In a large mixing bowl, combine the sliced apples, granulated sugar, brown sugar, flour, cinnamon, nutmeg, and lemon juice. Toss until the apples are evenly coated.
Pour the apple filling into the prepared pie crust and spread it out evenly.

For the Pecan Crumble Topping:

In a separate mixing bowl, combine the flour, brown sugar, chopped pecans, and melted butter. Mix until the ingredients are well combined and form a crumbly mixture.
Sprinkle the pecan crumble topping evenly over the apple filling in the pie crust. Cover the edges of the pie crust with aluminum foil to prevent them from over-browning.
Place the pie on a baking sheet to catch any drips, and bake in the preheated oven for 40-45 minutes, or until the filling is bubbly and the pecan crumble topping is golden brown.
Remove the pie from the oven and let it cool on a wire rack before serving.
Serve the pecan crumble apple pie warm or at room temperature, optionally with a scoop of vanilla ice cream or a dollop of whipped cream.

Enjoy this delicious pecan crumble apple pie as a comforting dessert for any occasion!

Macadamia Nut-Crusted Fish

Ingredients:

- 4 fish fillets (such as mahi-mahi, snapper, or cod)
- 1 cup macadamia nuts, finely chopped or crushed
- 1/2 cup panko breadcrumbs (optional, for extra crunch)
- 1/4 cup all-purpose flour
- 2 eggs, beaten
- Salt and pepper, to taste
- Olive oil or cooking spray
- Lemon wedges, for serving

Instructions:

Preheat your oven to 400°F (200°C). Line a baking sheet with parchment paper or lightly grease it with olive oil or cooking spray.

Season the fish fillets with salt and pepper on both sides.

Set up a breading station with three shallow dishes: one containing the all-purpose flour, one containing the beaten eggs, and one containing a mixture of the finely chopped macadamia nuts and panko breadcrumbs (if using).

Dredge each fish fillet in the flour, shaking off any excess. Then dip it into the beaten eggs, allowing any excess to drip off. Finally, press the fish fillet into the macadamia nut and breadcrumb mixture, coating it evenly on both sides.

Place the coated fish fillets onto the prepared baking sheet.

Drizzle a little olive oil over the top of each fish fillet, or lightly spray them with cooking spray. This will help the crust to brown nicely in the oven.

Bake the fish in the preheated oven for 12-15 minutes, or until the crust is golden brown and the fish is cooked through. The cooking time may vary depending on the thickness of the fish fillets.

Once cooked, remove the fish from the oven and let it rest for a few minutes before serving.

Serve the macadamia nut-crusted fish hot, garnished with lemon wedges on the side for squeezing over the top.

Enjoy this delicious and flavorful macadamia nut-crusted fish as a main course for a special dinner or any day of the week! It pairs well with a side of rice, steamed vegetables, or a fresh salad.

Sunflower Seed Salad Dressing

Ingredients:

- 1/2 cup raw sunflower seeds
- 1/4 cup water
- 2 tablespoons lemon juice
- 2 tablespoons apple cider vinegar
- 1 tablespoon honey or maple syrup (for sweetness, optional)
- 1 clove garlic, minced (optional)
- 1/2 teaspoon salt
- 1/4 teaspoon ground black pepper
- 1/4 cup extra-virgin olive oil

Instructions:

> In a blender or food processor, combine the raw sunflower seeds, water, lemon juice, apple cider vinegar, honey or maple syrup (if using), minced garlic (if using), salt, and pepper.
>
> Blend the ingredients on high speed until smooth and creamy, scraping down the sides of the blender or food processor as needed to ensure everything is well incorporated.
>
> With the blender or food processor running on low speed, gradually drizzle in the extra-virgin olive oil until the dressing emulsifies and thickens.
>
> Taste the dressing and adjust the seasoning as needed, adding more salt, pepper, lemon juice, or sweetener to suit your preferences.
>
> If the dressing is too thick, you can thin it out with a little more water or lemon juice until you reach the desired consistency.
>
> Once the dressing is ready, transfer it to a jar or container with a tight-fitting lid and refrigerate it until ready to use. The dressing will thicken slightly as it chills, so you may need to stir or shake it well before serving.
>
> Serve the sunflower seed salad dressing over your favorite salads, grain bowls, or vegetable dishes. Enjoy!

This sunflower seed salad dressing is not only delicious but also packed with healthy fats, vitamins, and minerals from the sunflower seeds. It adds a creamy and nutty flavor to your salads while being vegan-friendly and gluten-free.

Pistachio Crusted Salmon

Ingredients:

- 4 salmon fillets, skin-on or skinless (about 6 ounces each)
- 1 cup shelled pistachios, finely chopped
- 2 tablespoons Dijon mustard
- 2 tablespoons honey or maple syrup
- 1 tablespoon lemon juice
- 1 teaspoon lemon zest
- Salt and pepper, to taste
- Olive oil, for drizzling

Instructions:

Preheat your oven to 375°F (190°C). Line a baking sheet with parchment paper or lightly grease it with olive oil.
In a mixing bowl, combine the finely chopped pistachios, Dijon mustard, honey or maple syrup, lemon juice, lemon zest, salt, and pepper. Mix until well combined.
Pat the salmon fillets dry with paper towels and season them lightly with salt and pepper on both sides.
Place the salmon fillets on the prepared baking sheet, leaving a little space between each fillet.
Spoon the pistachio mixture evenly over the top of each salmon fillet, pressing gently to adhere the crust to the fish.
Drizzle a little olive oil over the top of each salmon fillet to help the crust brown nicely in the oven.
Bake the salmon in the preheated oven for 12-15 minutes, or until the pistachio crust is golden brown and the salmon is cooked through. The cooking time may vary depending on the thickness of the salmon fillets.
Once cooked, remove the salmon from the oven and let it rest for a few minutes before serving.
Serve the pistachio-crusted salmon hot, garnished with lemon wedges and fresh herbs if desired.

Enjoy this flavorful and elegant pistachio-crusted salmon as a main course for a special dinner or any day of the week! It pairs well with a side of roasted vegetables, quinoa, or a fresh green salad.

Sesame Seed Chicken Tenders

Ingredients:

- 1 lb chicken breast tenders or chicken breast, cut into strips
- 1/2 cup all-purpose flour
- 2 eggs, beaten
- 1 cup breadcrumbs (you can use panko breadcrumbs for extra crunch)
- 1/4 cup sesame seeds
- 1 teaspoon garlic powder
- 1 teaspoon onion powder
- 1/2 teaspoon salt
- 1/4 teaspoon black pepper
- Cooking oil, for frying
- Optional: dipping sauce of your choice (such as sweet chili sauce or soy sauce)

Instructions:

Preheat your oven to 375°F (190°C). Line a baking sheet with parchment paper. In a shallow dish, mix together the breadcrumbs, sesame seeds, garlic powder, onion powder, salt, and black pepper.

Set up a breading station with three shallow dishes: one containing the all-purpose flour, one containing the beaten eggs, and one containing the breadcrumb mixture.

Dredge each chicken tender in the flour, shaking off any excess. Then dip it into the beaten eggs, allowing any excess to drip off. Finally, coat it in the breadcrumb mixture, pressing gently to adhere the breadcrumbs and sesame seeds to the chicken.

Place the breaded chicken tenders onto the prepared baking sheet.

If you prefer baked chicken tenders, you can spray or brush them lightly with cooking oil before baking. Bake in the preheated oven for 18-20 minutes, or until golden brown and cooked through.

If you prefer fried chicken tenders, heat cooking oil in a large skillet over medium heat. Once the oil is hot, add the breaded chicken tenders in batches and cook for 3-4 minutes on each side, or until golden brown and cooked through. Transfer the cooked chicken tenders to a plate lined with paper towels to drain excess oil.

Serve the sesame seed chicken tenders hot with your favorite dipping sauce on the side.

Enjoy these crispy and flavorful sesame seed chicken tenders as a delicious snack, appetizer, or main course! They're sure to be a hit with family and friends.

Pine Nut Hummus

Ingredients:

- 1 can (15 ounces) chickpeas (garbanzo beans), drained and rinsed
- 1/4 cup pine nuts, plus extra for garnish
- 2 cloves garlic, minced
- 3 tablespoons tahini
- 3 tablespoons fresh lemon juice
- 2 tablespoons extra-virgin olive oil, plus extra for drizzling
- 1/2 teaspoon ground cumin
- 1/4 teaspoon paprika, plus extra for garnish
- Salt, to taste
- Water, as needed
- Fresh parsley or cilantro, for garnish (optional)

Instructions:

In a food processor, combine the drained and rinsed chickpeas, pine nuts, minced garlic, tahini, lemon juice, olive oil, ground cumin, paprika, and a pinch of salt. Process the mixture until smooth and creamy, scraping down the sides of the food processor as needed. If the hummus is too thick, you can add water, 1 tablespoon at a time, until you reach your desired consistency.
Taste the hummus and adjust the seasoning as needed, adding more salt or lemon juice if desired.
Transfer the pine nut hummus to a serving bowl and drizzle with a little extra-virgin olive oil. Sprinkle with some additional pine nuts and a pinch of paprika for garnish.
If desired, garnish the hummus with fresh parsley or cilantro for a pop of color and freshness.
Serve the pine nut hummus with pita bread, fresh vegetables, crackers, or chips for dipping.
Store any leftover hummus in an airtight container in the refrigerator for up to 5 days.

Enjoy this creamy and flavorful pine nut hummus as a tasty appetizer or snack! It's perfect for serving at parties, gatherings, or as a healthy spread for sandwiches and wraps.

Brazil Nut Crusted Pork Chops

Ingredients:

- 4 boneless pork chops
- 1 cup Brazil nuts, finely chopped
- 1/2 cup breadcrumbs (panko or regular)
- 2 tablespoons Dijon mustard
- 1 tablespoon honey or maple syrup
- 1 tablespoon olive oil
- 1 teaspoon dried thyme
- Salt and pepper, to taste
- Cooking spray or additional olive oil for greasing

Instructions:

Preheat your oven to 375°F (190°C). Prepare a baking dish by lightly greasing it with cooking spray or olive oil.

In a shallow bowl or plate, mix together the finely chopped Brazil nuts, breadcrumbs, dried thyme, salt, and pepper.

In another shallow bowl, whisk together the Dijon mustard, honey or maple syrup, and olive oil.

Pat the pork chops dry with paper towels and season them with salt and pepper on both sides.

Dip each pork chop into the Dijon mustard mixture, coating both sides evenly.

Press each pork chop into the Brazil nut and breadcrumb mixture, coating it well on both sides and pressing gently to adhere the crust.

Place the coated pork chops in the prepared baking dish.

Bake the pork chops in the preheated oven for 20-25 minutes, or until the internal temperature reaches 145°F (63°C) for medium-rare or 160°F (71°C) for medium, using a meat thermometer to check for doneness.

Once cooked through and golden brown, remove the pork chops from the oven and let them rest for a few minutes before serving.

Serve the Brazil nut-crusted pork chops hot with your favorite sides, such as roasted vegetables, mashed potatoes, or a fresh salad.

Enjoy these flavorful and crunchy pork chops as a delicious and satisfying meal!

Pumpkin Seed Pesto Pasta

Ingredients:

- 12 ounces (about 340g) pasta of your choice (such as spaghetti, linguine, or penne)
- 1 cup packed fresh basil leaves
- 1/2 cup roasted pumpkin seeds (pepitas)
- 2 cloves garlic, peeled
- 1/2 cup grated Parmesan cheese (or nutritional yeast for a vegan option)
- 1/4 cup extra-virgin olive oil
- 1 tablespoon fresh lemon juice
- Salt and pepper, to taste
- Optional toppings: extra grated Parmesan cheese, chopped fresh basil, roasted pumpkin seeds

Instructions:

Cook the pasta according to the package instructions until al dente. Reserve about 1/2 cup of pasta cooking water, then drain the pasta and set it aside.
In a food processor or blender, combine the fresh basil leaves, roasted pumpkin seeds, garlic cloves, and grated Parmesan cheese. Pulse until the ingredients are finely chopped and well combined.
With the food processor or blender running, gradually drizzle in the extra-virgin olive oil and fresh lemon juice until the mixture forms a smooth and creamy pesto sauce. If the pesto is too thick, you can add a little bit of the reserved pasta cooking water to thin it out.
Season the pumpkin seed pesto with salt and pepper to taste, adjusting the seasoning as needed.
In a large mixing bowl, toss the cooked pasta with the pumpkin seed pesto until the pasta is evenly coated.
Serve the pumpkin seed pesto pasta hot, garnished with extra grated Parmesan cheese, chopped fresh basil, and roasted pumpkin seeds if desired.

Enjoy this flavorful and nutritious pumpkin seed pesto pasta as a satisfying meal! You can customize it by adding grilled chicken, roasted vegetables, or your favorite protein for extra flavor and texture.

Almond Flour Pizza Crust

Ingredients:

- 2 cups almond flour
- 2 large eggs
- 2 tablespoons olive oil
- 1 teaspoon baking powder
- 1/2 teaspoon garlic powder
- 1/2 teaspoon dried oregano
- 1/2 teaspoon salt
- Optional toppings: pizza sauce, cheese, vegetables, meats, herbs, etc.

Instructions:

Preheat your oven to 375°F (190°C). Line a baking sheet with parchment paper. In a large mixing bowl, combine the almond flour, baking powder, garlic powder, dried oregano, and salt. Mix well to ensure that the ingredients are evenly distributed.

In a separate bowl, whisk together the eggs and olive oil until well combined. Pour the wet ingredients into the dry ingredients and mix until a dough forms. Use your hands to knead the dough until it comes together and is uniform in texture.

Place the dough ball onto the prepared baking sheet. Use your hands to press and shape the dough into a round pizza crust, spreading it out evenly to your desired thickness. You can make the edges slightly thicker for a crusty edge.

Bake the pizza crust in the preheated oven for 10-12 minutes, or until it starts to turn golden brown around the edges.

Remove the crust from the oven and let it cool for a few minutes. At this point, you can add your desired toppings.

Once you've added your toppings, return the pizza to the oven and bake for an additional 10-12 minutes, or until the cheese is melted and bubbly, and the crust is golden brown and cooked through.

Remove the pizza from the oven and let it cool for a few minutes before slicing and serving.

Enjoy your delicious homemade almond flour pizza with your favorite toppings! It's a nutritious and satisfying option for pizza lovers who are looking for a healthier alternative.

Walnut Encrusted Goat Cheese Balls

Ingredients:

- 8 ounces (about 225g) goat cheese, softened
- 1 cup walnuts, finely chopped
- 1/4 cup all-purpose flour
- 1 large egg, beaten
- 1 tablespoon honey
- Pinch of salt
- Pinch of black pepper
- Olive oil, for frying (or you can bake them if preferred)
- Optional: honey, for drizzling

Instructions:

Place the finely chopped walnuts in a shallow bowl or plate. Set aside.
In another shallow bowl, whisk together the beaten egg, honey, salt, and black pepper until well combined.
Shape the softened goat cheese into small balls, about 1 tablespoon each.
Roll each goat cheese ball in the all-purpose flour, shaking off any excess.
Dip each floured goat cheese ball into the egg mixture, coating it evenly.
Roll the coated goat cheese ball in the chopped walnuts, pressing gently to adhere the nuts to the cheese.
Place the walnut-encrusted goat cheese balls on a plate or baking sheet lined with parchment paper. If you're not serving them immediately, you can refrigerate them for about 30 minutes to firm up.
To fry the goat cheese balls, heat olive oil in a skillet over medium heat. Once the oil is hot, carefully add the goat cheese balls in batches, making sure not to overcrowd the pan. Fry for about 1-2 minutes per side, or until golden brown and crispy. Transfer the fried goat cheese balls to a plate lined with paper towels to drain any excess oil.
Alternatively, if you prefer to bake the goat cheese balls, preheat your oven to 375°F (190°C). Place the walnut-encrusted goat cheese balls on a baking sheet lined with parchment paper and bake for 10-12 minutes, or until lightly golden brown and heated through.
Serve the walnut-encrusted goat cheese balls hot, optionally drizzled with honey for extra sweetness.

Enjoy these delicious and elegant walnut-encrusted goat cheese balls as a delightful appetizer or snack at your next gathering or party! They're sure to impress your guests with their creamy texture and crunchy coating.

Cashew Alfredo Sauce

Ingredients:

- 1 cup raw cashews, soaked in water for at least 4 hours or overnight
- 2 cloves garlic, minced
- 1 tablespoon olive oil
- 1 cup vegetable broth or water
- 1/4 cup nutritional yeast
- 2 tablespoons lemon juice
- 1 teaspoon onion powder
- 1/2 teaspoon garlic powder
- Salt and pepper, to taste
- Optional: chopped fresh parsley, for garnish

Instructions:

Drain and rinse the soaked cashews thoroughly under cold water.

In a skillet, heat the olive oil over medium heat. Add the minced garlic and sauté for 1-2 minutes, or until fragrant.

In a blender or food processor, combine the soaked cashews, sautéed garlic, vegetable broth or water, nutritional yeast, lemon juice, onion powder, garlic powder, salt, and pepper.

Blend the ingredients on high speed until smooth and creamy, scraping down the sides of the blender or food processor as needed to ensure everything is well combined. If the sauce is too thick, you can add a little more vegetable broth or water to reach your desired consistency.

Once the sauce is smooth and creamy, taste and adjust the seasoning as needed, adding more salt, pepper, or lemon juice to suit your preferences.

If using the sauce with pasta, you can toss it with cooked pasta directly in the skillet over low heat until heated through, or simply pour it over your cooked pasta.

Serve the cashew Alfredo sauce hot, garnished with chopped fresh parsley if desired.

Enjoy this creamy and flavorful cashew Alfredo sauce as a delicious topping for pasta, vegetables, or any other dish that calls for Alfredo sauce. It's a versatile and dairy-free option that's sure to please everyone at the table!

Coconut Flour Fried Chicken

Ingredients:

- 4 boneless, skinless chicken breasts (or chicken tenders)
- 1/2 cup coconut flour
- 2 eggs
- 1/4 cup milk (or non-dairy milk of your choice)
- 1 cup shredded unsweetened coconut
- 1 teaspoon garlic powder
- 1 teaspoon onion powder
- 1 teaspoon paprika
- 1/2 teaspoon salt
- 1/4 teaspoon black pepper
- Cooking oil, for frying (such as coconut oil or vegetable oil)

Instructions:

In a shallow bowl, whisk together the eggs and milk to create an egg wash. Set aside.

In another shallow bowl, combine the coconut flour, shredded coconut, garlic powder, onion powder, paprika, salt, and black pepper. Mix well to combine.

Dip each chicken breast (or chicken tender) into the coconut flour mixture, coating it evenly on all sides. Shake off any excess flour mixture.

Next, dip the coated chicken into the egg wash, ensuring that it's fully coated. Finally, dip the chicken back into the coconut flour mixture, pressing gently to adhere the coconut flour and shredded coconut to the chicken.

Repeat the breading process with the remaining chicken breasts (or chicken tenders).

Heat cooking oil in a large skillet over medium heat. You'll want enough oil to come up about halfway up the sides of the chicken pieces.

Once the oil is hot, carefully add the breaded chicken to the skillet, making sure not to overcrowd the pan. Cook the chicken for 4-5 minutes on each side, or until golden brown and cooked through. The internal temperature should reach 165°F (74°C) for chicken breasts or 170°F (77°C) for chicken tenders.

Once cooked, transfer the chicken to a plate lined with paper towels to drain any excess oil.

Serve the coconut flour fried chicken hot, alongside your favorite dipping sauce or with a side of vegetables or salad.

Enjoy this crispy and flavorful coconut flour fried chicken as a delicious and healthier alternative to traditional fried chicken!

Hazelnut-Crusted Tofu

Ingredients:

- 1 block (about 14-16 ounces) firm or extra-firm tofu
- 1/2 cup raw hazelnuts
- 1/4 cup breadcrumbs (optional, for extra crunch)
- 2 tablespoons all-purpose flour or cornstarch
- 1 teaspoon garlic powder
- 1 teaspoon onion powder
- 1/2 teaspoon smoked paprika (optional)
- Salt and pepper, to taste
- 2 tablespoons soy sauce or tamari
- 2 tablespoons maple syrup or agave nectar
- 1 tablespoon olive oil or cooking spray

Instructions:

Preheat your oven to 400°F (200°C). Line a baking sheet with parchment paper or lightly grease it with olive oil or cooking spray.

Press the tofu: Place the block of tofu between clean kitchen towels or paper towels, and place a heavy object on top (such as a cast-iron skillet or a few heavy books). Press the tofu for about 20-30 minutes to remove excess moisture.

While the tofu is pressing, prepare the hazelnut crust. In a food processor or blender, pulse the raw hazelnuts until finely chopped. Be careful not to over-process, as you want a coarse texture, similar to breadcrumbs. Transfer the chopped hazelnuts to a shallow bowl or plate.

Add breadcrumbs (if using), all-purpose flour or cornstarch, garlic powder, onion powder, smoked paprika (if using), salt, and pepper to the bowl with the chopped hazelnuts. Mix well to combine.

In another shallow bowl, whisk together soy sauce or tamari and maple syrup or agave nectar to create a marinade.

Once the tofu is pressed, cut it into slices or cubes, depending on your preference.

Dip each tofu piece into the marinade, coating it evenly on all sides.

Next, dip the tofu into the hazelnut crust mixture, pressing gently to coat it thoroughly with the hazelnut mixture.

Place the coated tofu pieces onto the prepared baking sheet.

Drizzle or spray the top of the tofu pieces with olive oil or cooking spray to help them crisp up in the oven.

Bake the hazelnut-crusted tofu in the preheated oven for 20-25 minutes, flipping halfway through, or until the crust is golden brown and crispy.
Once cooked, remove the tofu from the oven and let it cool for a few minutes before serving.

Serve the hazelnut-crusted tofu hot as a delicious main dish or appetizer, alongside your favorite dipping sauce or on top of salads or grain bowls. Enjoy the crunchy texture and nutty flavor of this delightful dish!

Pecan-Crusted Eggplant

Ingredients:

- 1 large eggplant, sliced into 1/2-inch rounds
- 1 cup pecans, finely chopped
- 1/2 cup breadcrumbs (optional, for extra crunch)
- 2 eggs, beaten
- 1/4 cup all-purpose flour or cornstarch
- 1 teaspoon garlic powder
- 1 teaspoon onion powder
- 1/2 teaspoon smoked paprika (optional)
- Salt and pepper, to taste
- Olive oil or cooking spray

Instructions:

Preheat your oven to 400°F (200°C). Line a baking sheet with parchment paper or lightly grease it with olive oil or cooking spray.

Slice the eggplant into 1/2-inch rounds. If desired, you can peel the eggplant before slicing, although this is optional.

In a shallow bowl or plate, combine the finely chopped pecans, breadcrumbs (if using), all-purpose flour or cornstarch, garlic powder, onion powder, smoked paprika (if using), salt, and pepper. Mix well to combine.

In another shallow bowl, beat the eggs to create an egg wash.

Dip each eggplant round into the egg wash, coating it evenly on all sides.

Next, dip the eggplant into the pecan mixture, pressing gently to coat it thoroughly with the pecan mixture.

Place the coated eggplant rounds onto the prepared baking sheet.

Drizzle or spray the top of the eggplant rounds with olive oil or cooking spray to help them crisp up in the oven.

Bake the pecan-crusted eggplant in the preheated oven for 20-25 minutes, flipping halfway through, or until the crust is golden brown and crispy.

Once cooked, remove the eggplant from the oven and let it cool for a few minutes before serving.

Serve the pecan-crusted eggplant hot as a delicious appetizer, side dish, or main course.

Enjoy the crunchy texture and nutty flavor of this delightful dish! You can also serve it with your favorite dipping sauce or alongside a salad for a complete meal.

Macadamia Nut Salad Toppings

Ingredients:

- Macadamia nuts
- Optional: sugar, honey, maple syrup, olive oil, lemon juice, garlic, herbs, coconut flakes, oats, Parmesan cheese, salt

Recipes:

Toasted Macadamia Nuts:
- Whole or chopped macadamia nuts
- Heat a dry skillet over medium heat.
- Add macadamia nuts and toast for a few minutes until fragrant and lightly golden brown.
- Sprinkle over salads for a delicious crunch.

Candied Macadamia Nuts:
- Whole or chopped macadamia nuts
- Sugar
- Water
- Preheat oven to 350°F (175°C).
- In a bowl, mix sugar and water until dissolved.
- Toss macadamia nuts in the sugar mixture.
- Spread nuts on a baking sheet and bake for 10-15 minutes until caramelized.
- Cool and use as a sweet topping for salads.

Macadamia Nut Dressing:
- Macadamia nuts
- Olive oil
- Lemon juice
- Garlic
- Herbs (such as basil or parsley)
- Salt
- Blend all ingredients until smooth and creamy.
- Drizzle over salads for a rich and flavorful dressing.

Macadamia Nut Brittle:
- Whole macadamia nuts
- Sugar
- Preheat oven to 350°F (175°C).

- In a saucepan, heat sugar until melted and golden.
- Stir in macadamia nuts and pour onto a baking sheet.
- Let cool, then break into pieces and sprinkle over salads.

Macadamia Nut Crusted Chicken or Tofu:
- Macadamia nuts, crushed
- Chicken breasts or tofu
- Coat chicken or tofu in crushed macadamia nuts.
- Bake or pan-fry until golden brown and cooked through.
- Slice and serve on top of salads for added protein and flavor.

Sunflower Seed Encrusted Pork Tenderloin

Ingredients:

- 1 pork tenderloin (about 1 to 1.5 pounds)
- 1 cup raw sunflower seeds
- 2 tablespoons all-purpose flour
- 1 teaspoon garlic powder
- 1 teaspoon onion powder
- 1/2 teaspoon smoked paprika
- Salt and black pepper, to taste
- 2 tablespoons Dijon mustard
- 1 tablespoon honey or maple syrup
- Olive oil, for searing

Instructions:

Preheat your oven to 375°F (190°C).
Trim any excess fat or silver skin from the pork tenderloin, if necessary, and pat it dry with paper towels.
In a dry skillet over medium heat, toast the sunflower seeds for 3-4 minutes, stirring frequently, until lightly golden and fragrant. Remove from heat and let them cool slightly.
In a food processor or blender, pulse the toasted sunflower seeds until coarsely ground. Transfer the ground sunflower seeds to a shallow dish or plate.
In another shallow dish, combine the all-purpose flour, garlic powder, onion powder, smoked paprika, salt, and black pepper.
In a small bowl, mix together the Dijon mustard and honey (or maple syrup) to create a glaze.
Generously season the pork tenderloin with salt and black pepper.
Brush the pork tenderloin all over with the Dijon mustard glaze, ensuring it is evenly coated.
Roll the glazed pork tenderloin in the ground sunflower seeds, pressing gently to adhere the seeds to the surface.
Next, coat the pork tenderloin in the seasoned flour mixture, shaking off any excess flour.

In an oven-safe skillet or baking dish, heat a drizzle of olive oil over medium-high heat. Once hot, add the coated pork tenderloin and sear for 2-3 minutes on each side until golden brown.

Transfer the skillet or baking dish to the preheated oven and roast the pork tenderloin for 20-25 minutes, or until the internal temperature reaches 145°F (63°C) for medium-rare or 160°F (71°C) for medium.

Once cooked, remove the pork tenderloin from the oven and let it rest for a few minutes before slicing.

Slice the sunflower seed encrusted pork tenderloin into thick slices and serve hot. Enjoy the crispy exterior and juicy, flavorful interior of this delicious dish!

Pistachio Crusted Goat Cheese

Ingredients:

- 1 log (about 8 ounces) goat cheese, chilled
- 1 cup shelled pistachios, finely chopped
- 2 tablespoons honey
- 1 tablespoon Dijon mustard
- 1 teaspoon fresh thyme leaves (optional)
- Pinch of salt
- Pinch of black pepper
- Crackers, bread, or sliced baguette, for serving

Instructions:

Preheat your oven to 375°F (190°C).

Remove the chilled goat cheese log from the refrigerator and let it sit at room temperature for about 15-20 minutes to soften slightly.

In a shallow dish or plate, spread out the finely chopped pistachios.

In a small bowl, whisk together the honey, Dijon mustard, fresh thyme leaves (if using), salt, and black pepper until well combined.

Slice the goat cheese log into rounds, about 1/2-inch thick.

Dip each goat cheese round into the honey-mustard mixture, coating it evenly on all sides.

Next, roll the coated goat cheese round in the chopped pistachios, pressing gently to adhere the pistachios to the cheese.

Place the pistachio-crusted goat cheese rounds on a parchment-lined baking sheet or in an oven-safe dish.

Bake the goat cheese rounds in the preheated oven for 8-10 minutes, or until the pistachio crust is lightly golden and the cheese is warmed through.

Remove the pistachio-crusted goat cheese from the oven and let it cool for a few minutes before serving.

Serve the warm goat cheese rounds with crackers, bread, or sliced baguette for spreading. Enjoy the creamy, tangy goat cheese paired with the crunchy, nutty pistachio crust!

Sesame Seed Coated Shrimp

Ingredients:

- 1 pound large shrimp, peeled and deveined, tails left on
- 1/2 cup sesame seeds (white or black, or a combination of both)
- 1/4 cup all-purpose flour
- 2 eggs, beaten
- 1 teaspoon garlic powder
- 1 teaspoon onion powder
- 1/2 teaspoon paprika
- Salt and pepper, to taste
- Cooking oil, for frying
- Optional: dipping sauce of your choice (such as sweet chili sauce or soy sauce)

Instructions:

Rinse the shrimp under cold water and pat them dry with paper towels. Leave the tails on for a decorative presentation.

In a shallow dish, combine the sesame seeds, all-purpose flour, garlic powder, onion powder, paprika, salt, and pepper. Mix well to evenly distribute the spices.

In another shallow dish, beat the eggs until well combined.

Dip each shrimp into the beaten eggs, allowing any excess to drip off.

Next, coat each shrimp in the sesame seed mixture, pressing gently to ensure the seeds adhere to the shrimp.

Place the coated shrimp on a plate or baking sheet lined with parchment paper. Repeat the process with the remaining shrimp.

Heat cooking oil in a large skillet over medium-high heat. You'll want enough oil to come up about halfway up the sides of the shrimp.

Once the oil is hot, carefully add the coated shrimp to the skillet in batches, making sure not to overcrowd the pan. Fry for about 2-3 minutes on each side, or until the shrimp are golden brown and crispy.

Using a slotted spoon, transfer the fried shrimp to a plate lined with paper towels to drain any excess oil.

Serve the sesame seed coated shrimp hot with your favorite dipping sauce on the side.

Enjoy these crispy and flavorful sesame seed coated shrimp as a delicious appetizer or main dish! They're sure to be a hit at any gathering or dinner table.

www.ingramcontent.com/pod-product-compliance
Lightning Source LLC
LaVergne TN
LVHW081614060526
838201LV00054B/2251